Old Maid
Is a
Dirty Word

Cover and illustrations by Kevin Davidson.

Design by Mary Johnson.

Photography by George Stabler.

Old Maid Is a Dirty Word
Judy Downs Douglass

Campus Crusade for Christ International

To my mother and father

Contents

foreword

i'm ann, single, and 30 years old. when judy downs douglass sent me her manuscript, *Old Maid Is a Dirty Word,* i read it with tremendous enthusiasm and interest.

if you are single — male or female — or if you are interested in our struggles, you will love this book.

it is honest, fresh, to the point, realistic. there is comfort, identification, feeling AND the dare to feel perfectly whole and happy without a mate. i believe in her words . . . they are so biblical and have been so true for me.

have you ever met judy?

she is intelligent, vibrant and lovely. it's a whole part of her, inside and out. AND she was that way before she married steve at 31. she is determined and dynamic in such an uncomplicated way. you'll see as you read.

ann kiemel
boston, massachusetts

Introduction

On June 8, 1975, at the age of 31, I married Stephen B. Douglass. That was an exciting day for me! But it is probably enough to make you put this book down and say, "Another married woman telling me how wonderful it is to be single? No thanks." I know. That's what I would have done.

But wait! Let me tell you about this little book. I wrote it while I was 26 to 29 years of age, as I went through many personal struggles. I shared this book with a number of friends, who said it was helpful to them and encouraged me to publish it.

So I began to make some efforts toward publication. But then I became engaged and, because of lack of time and because I feel married women shouldn't write books on being single, I put the book away.

During our first year of marriage, however, my husband encouraged me to publish my book. I pulled it out and read through it again, and was delighted to find that I still felt the principles I had proposed were true. I saw no content I wanted to change.

Although *Old Maid Is A Dirty Word* is being published by a married woman, it was written by a single woman for single women. I hope you will find what it has to say as helpful in exploring and living your single life as it was for me.

Judy Downs Douglass

1/ A Quarter of a Century

"A quarter of a century. I'll be a quarter of a century old tomorrow and no man in sight."

It was coffee break and one of the girls in the office was bewailing her upcoming 25th birthday. Single and 21 is swinging, but single and 25 is fast approaching old maidhood.

When I was 23, a 28-year-old friend of mine got married. I remember thinking with horror, as I sat watching the ceremony, "I would just die if I didn't get married until I was 28. I don't think I could stand it."

Well, I've passed 28, and I am still single and surviving and enjoying it.* I have even lived through the weddings of both my younger sisters.

But I have not always enjoyed being single. And for most of us, it is difficult to stay single and satisfied. We have

---

See introduction for explanation for my use of present tense concerning singleness.

so many pressures to contend with as our own normal desires to love and be loved constantly clamor for fulfillment.

One girl admitted, "Basically I'm happy being single, but there are times I do feel that I have been left out."

"Sometimes I enjoy being single and sometimes I hate it," a 26-year-old woman said. "Lately I have had an increasingly strong desire to get married, and it is a continuous battle not to get depressed."

Another girl added, "Occasionally I just desire the intimate relationship I would have with a husband."

Then there is the social pressure that attacks as all our friends get married and we begin to feel left out. Especially when the kid we used to babysit for has a baby.

As one girl put it, "The time that I feel incomplete is when society subtly implies that I am a social zero since I am unmarried. If I go to a party and all my friends are married, where do I fit in?"

If the implied pressure isn't enough, there are the direct questions: "Why aren't you married?" "You're not getting any younger, you know." "How come a pretty girl like you hasn't been snatched up by some young man?" "Maybe you shouldn't be so choosy." "Have you tried *this* to get him to propose?"

It's not surprising, then, that many girls find themselves echoing the sentiments expressed in this poem by some anonymous woman:

UNKNOWN MAN

Oh, unknown man, whose rib I am,
    why don't you come for me?
A lonely, homesick rib I am
    that would with others be.
I want to wed — there, now, 'tis said!
    (I won't deny and fib.)
I want my man to come at once
    and claim his rib!

Some men have thought that I'd be theirs,
  but only for a bit;
We found out soon it wouldn't do —
  we didn't seem to fit.
There's just one place, the only space
  I'll fit (I will not fib).
I want that man to come at once
  and claim his rib!

Oh, don't you sometimes feel a lack,
  a new rib needed there?
It's I! Do come and get me soon
  before I have gray hair.
Come get me dear! I'm homesick here!
  I want (and I'll not fib).
I want my man to come at once
  And claim his rib.

It was while I was in the midst of just such thoughts that I was asked to speak to some single women about "attitudes toward marriage." But I realized that I didn't have problems with my attitudes toward marriage. I *wanted* to get married. My attitudes toward being single were the problem.

My attempts to define and deal with these attitudes led to this book. I have tried to include many practical "how to's" for overcoming the problems of singleness, but my main focus has been on attitudes. For I've found that when I have the right attitude — that is, when I can look at a situation from God's perspective — the "problems" generally tend to disappear. Perhaps you'll find that you identify with some of these attitudes, and hopefully you will also be able to discover God's perspective on them.

2/ "The Bravest Girl in the World"

You're not an old maid if you have ever been asked, I've been told. So at times, when I've been tempted to relegate myself to that position, I take comfort in the fact that I have been asked.

I have even been engaged. That's how I became the bravest girl in the world. I called off my engagement just a few weeks before the wedding.

I dated this fellow for four years — all through college. In my senior year, we decided to get married. I was excited; I wanted to get married and I loved him very much.

More than anything else, though, I wanted God's perfect will for my life, and there were things about our relationship that made me question whether this was really what God had in store for me.

I wanted my marriage to be beautiful, and the beautiful marriages I had seen were ones in which the husband was the leader, especially in spiritual things.

That wasn't true in my relationship with my fiancé. His interest in God had developed and continued largely to please me, I felt. And he didn't seem to truly share my desire to be completely available to God to do whatever He wanted.

I also believed that God had given me some talents and training I could use in serving Him, and it didn't seem as though marrying this young man would enable me to really develop these abilities.

Many times during our engagement I had said to God: "Lord, I want what You want for me. If this marriage isn't Your will, then You tell me and You stop it." Yet, I sensed no change of direction from God.

Then, just a few weeks before the wedding, I began to have questions. I felt that God was working in my heart to convince me that I wasn't to marry this man.

I argued with Him about it: "Lord, You've had many chances to tell me this marriage was wrong. It's too late to call it off now. Everything's ready."

Slowly He brought me around to the point where I could say that I was willing to call it off if that was what He wanted. Even that wasn't enough. I had to completely yield my will to His will. So finally I said, "I am not going to get married."

At that moment I was flooded with peace — a greater peace than I have ever before experienced — and I knew that I had made the right decision.

Of course, my friends and my family were startled, shocked, bewildered. They couldn't understand why. But many of them told me that I was the bravest girl they knew. They didn't think they could have called it off.

Why was it a brave thing to do? Why, when a girl calls off her wedding, do other girls consider her courageous?

First, it means that you are willing to admit, "I made a mistake." It is always difficult and embarrassing to say you are wrong, especially when the wedding invitations are already out. But that is preferable to making the much bigger and more disastrous mistake of marrying the wrong person.

It also means you are willing to face all the questions and doubts of your friends and family. One friend asked, "If you didn't know after four years, how can you *ever* be sure?" My family said, "Why did you wait so long?" I couldn't answer them.

And of course it is always painful to hurt someone, especially someone you love. The pain I was causing my fiancé was so unbearable to me that I almost married him anyway. Then a friend reminded me that, just as I was showing my willingness to trust God with my life, so I needed to trust Him with my fiancé's life.

But the greatest reason it is brave to break an engagement is that it means you are willing to let one go in hopes of something even better. You are willing to take a chance that you will get another chance.

For example, a fellow I dated several years later said his respect for me increased when he learned I had broken an engagement. To him, it meant that I wasn't so anxious to get married that I grabbed the first man I could catch.

In reality, though, bravery has little to do with it. In my situation, I was saying to God, "I trust You. I believe that You know what You are doing and that You want the very best for me."

This was an important lesson for me in my growth as a Christian. I realized that, as long as I truly wanted God's perfect will and was willing to do whatever God wanted, He would continually guide me in the way I should go.

He also confirmed my faith that He would take care of my fiancé. When I saw him two years later, he said, "The greatest thing that happened in my life was meeting you, for as a result I received Christ into my life. The second greatest thing was your breaking up with me, because then I began to become the man God wanted me to be."

In spite of the spiritual lessons I learned, however, I couldn't help eating up the talk about how brave I was.

I became convinced that, of course, God would bring the right one along soon to reward my courage and trust. One very mature Christian woman tried to console me: "I'm sure that God will bring him soon, after what you've done and been through."

3/ "Every Girl Is Entitled to a Husband"

Convinced of my courage and certain that God owed me a man, I found myself falling into an attitude that most single girls deny they have, but which they actually practice. It is the attitude that every girl is entitled to a husband.

After all, we think, that's part of the plan, isn't it? It's the way society operates. Marriage and the family are the foundation on which the world's social structure is built.

Despite the fact that many sociological prophets have forecast the final days for the family, and that unmarried couples living together are no longer a rarity, most girls still want to get married, and even assume that marriage is their right and privilege.

That's exactly what we are brought up to believe. Nearly everything we do in life seems to prepare us to be wives. We play with dolls. We learn to cook and sew and clean. We learn skills for jobs that are easy to leave when a husband or baby comes along.

And, of course, we eagerly anticipate the day when that man does come along. We want to serve him and love him and please him. We desire the security and love he will give us. Our whole lives and thought processes tend to revolve around getting ready for marriage.

But it's not just our social system that operates on marriage. God's Word teaches that the family is part of the plan. God made woman for man. The Bible says, "Therefore shall a man leave his father and mother and shall cleave unto his wife and they shall be one flesh."

On the surface, it seems that a girl has every right to believe she is entitled to a husband. Most of the women I've talked to think so:

"It seems logical to me that every girl should have a husband," stated one young woman. "After all, every girl I know wants to get married just as I do."

"If a girl desires to get married, then God will give her the desires of her heart."

And, "Although I see convincing evidence to the contrary, I really doubt that it's God's will for any woman not to be married."

We just don't want to face the reality that not all women get married. Logistically, it's not possible — there are more women than men in the world.

Most girls, however, will get married. It *is* the way society operates and it *is* part of God's plan. There are some, however, who will not. And most of us are unwilling to admit that we might be one of the ones who doesn't.

One girl stated emphatically, "It is part of the plan. That's what we're here for — to get married and have a family. God wants more Christian families."

"I won't be fulfilled unless I'm married," admitted another. "I need a man. Maybe some women don't need a man, but I have to have one before I'm going to be satisfied in life. I just can't live alone."

Some are sure their faith in God will weaken if marriage isn't in God's plan for them. "If I don't get married," said one, "I will undoubtedly become bitter toward God. I will feel that He has cheated me and not given me the fullest possible life."

Not so strong was this comment: "Gulp! I'm satisfied to be single today, but I can't help but believe that I'll be miserable if I'm single in my 40's or 80's."

I found myself thinking those same thoughts. When I realized that not everybody could get married, I refused to believe that I might be one who wouldn't. After all, I did deserve a husband, considering I was brave enough to give one up.

We all tend to think that we deserve to be happy — that God *owes* us happiness. To most of us that means a husband. I had to learn that everything I have is a gift from God. The Bible tells me that nothing good dwells in me. Therefore, I merit no favor from a God who is perfect. In myself I deserve nothing.

But God is also loving and chooses to give us many good things. One of those good things could be marriage. If we get married, it is because God has given us a husband as a gift — and that is His calling for us. But an equally good thing is singleness. If we don't get married, then that is our special calling — another wonderful gift from God.

4/ "I Know He's the One"

A young man I know well once remarked, "It's amazing how many girls have been sure that I was God's will for their lives."

Most girls go through at least one relationship in which they are sure "he's the one."

This is especially true when a girl has just become a Christian or committed her life to Christ. Then she starts dating a Christian guy, and the quality of the relationship is so much better than any she has had before that she is certain God is leading them toward marriage.

But it can happen to more mature Christians as well. You meet a guy who has all the desired qualities. Or he is the first man to offer real spiritual leadership. Or there is such communication and oneness of interest. Or a certain man has needs and strengths that complement your needs and strengths. These are all good things to have in a friendship — and a marriage relationship — and they aren't to be discounted. But too often we assume that these things lead to marriage. They don't always.

Sometimes a girl has no such spiritual reasons — she just wants to get married, and he's the closest man around. So she's sure he's "the one."

It happened to me. I was dating a fellow I really liked and I began to get a funny feeling — a feeling that he was "the one." I knew, from the experience of others, that funny feelings *could* be valid.

For example, one friend of mine met a guy when she was 14 and decided right then that he was God's partner for her. She didn't see him for many years, and in the meantime he became engaged to someone else. That didn't work out, and then God brought my friend and this man together in their work.

Even then he was dating someone else. But suddenly God seemed to hit him on the head, and he knew that she was the one. They got married six months later.

Another girl, one of my roommates, was convinced that a fellow she was dating occasionally was the one. She is now married to someone else, but her certainty at that time encouraged me to believe *my* funny feeling. I was determined that this young man and I were going to get married.

But I wanted to do this right. Others I knew had had many Bible verses to validate their funny feelings, so I began to read. Sure enough, I found some Scriptures that convinced me that, if I would wait for God's will, He was going to give me this man.

Probably the thing that most convinced me that I was right about my funny feeling, however, was that other people encouraged me. My friends said, "Oh you're just perfect together." "I think it's wonderful that you know he's the one."

It seemed that the ones who encouraged me most were the married women. Each would tell me how she had known that her husband was the right one and then urge me to simply trust God to bring us together.

Then the fellow quit dating me. Dismayed at first, I quickly rebounded. I vowed I could wait forever.

He became the center of my life. I developed a sort of radar, gravitating to where he was. And I was always available to run into him — especially outside his office.

I fixed my hair the way I knew he liked it. If he complimented a dress, I wore it frequently. I interpreted his slightest attention as renewed interest. And I had this romantic idea that, when he did fall in love with me, it would not be because I had won his love, but because God had given him that love for me.

I waited a year. Finally another guy came along and took my eyes off "the one." This, of course, confused me. If I was so sure that he was God's will for my life, how could I have been wrong? How could I *ever* know?

Often, when we really want something, we can convince ourselves that it is right for us to have that thing. For instance, God *does* use His Word to confirm His will to us, and I thought I was seeking His will in this relationship. But I was looking for confirmation of *my* will, not God's. I looked for verses that supported what I had already decided I wanted.

At the same time, it is possible for either person to feel confident that a relationship should lead to marriage before the other one is sure. But the other person has to know eventually. When it is right, both will have that confidence.

Since this "funny feeling" seems to be a common disease among single women, we would be wise to learn how to understand and deal with it.

We can put our funny feelings to good use. The "certainty" is often just a bad case of infatuation, which can be a blessing or a real pain to the man. A girl can be aggressive, making herself too available, and usually frightening most men from even keeping up a friendship.

Or she can employ her love for his benefit, praying often for him. I'm convinced that sometimes God allows a girl to have a crush on a guy because he needs someone to pray for him at that time.

A crush can also help us to understand more about our relationship with God. When my love has been unreturned, it hurts. That helps me realize how much God loves me, and how much I hurt Him when I don't return that love — by not really caring or by choosing my own way rather than His.

We need to learn not to rely on feelings, but rather to treat "funny feelings" carefully. A friend wrote me after her first year of marriage:

> I was a sucker for funny feelings for years. All my blunders and embarrassing downfalls made me so wary of funny feelings that, when the real thing came, I was suspicious of it.
>
> When I first met John, I wasn't overly impressed with him, but had an unmistakable 'feeling' that I was going to marry him. That scared me. Not that I didn't like him. I just didn't want to become a parasite to a funny feeling again, especially if it were false.
>
> So I didn't breathe a word of it for a long time. My actions toward John were far from aggressive. As I found myself falling in love with him, I withdrew even more. I wanted so much for that 'sense of the future' to be purely of God and not something I dreamed up and spread around so my married friends could nurture it the way they had so many other false hopes.
>
> I was careful of what I said when I did talk about it. I had learned that, the more you talk about a funny feeling, the more it is confirmed and the harder it will be to face its falsehood when the

time comes.

So my motivation for furthering a relationship with John was not based on a funny feeling, but on the fact that I enjoyed him and he enjoyed me, and that current friendship was all we both needed. God would have to deal with any feelings about the future.

When we did decide to get married, it was not because of that funny feeling, but because of a love that had grown and an assurance that this was God's choice.

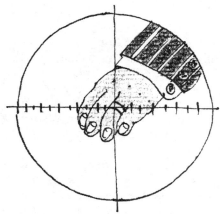

5/ "I Hope He's the One"

When we're not sure he's the one, then we at least *hope* so. We are forever peering around the next corner of our lives, hoping "he" is just ahead.

Every man we meet we evaluate: "Could I be interested in him? Would I like to marry him? Is he smart enough, tall enough, good-looking enough, rich enough? Can I get him to like me?"

I can remember, when meeting a guy, immediately looking to see if he were wearing a wedding ring.

Actually, though, we often think backwards in our approach to relationships. When we're dating someone we like, we assume (because we hope so) that he's the one until we find out that he's not. Therefore we *act* as if he's the one before we know he is.

This wrong-way approach can put the brakes on some going-places relationships. Men seem to have a built-in fear of being trapped. They think every single girl over 21 is out to get them.

And not without cause. That's often the impression we give — because it's usually true.

I hear girls complain, "It's impossible to have even a friendship with most guys. As soon as a relationship begins to develop, they run the other way."

The trouble is, our eagerness to change our names usually shows. So we make it hard to have close friendships with men.

I can remember two relationships I ruined. In both cases, after just a few dates, my "hope so" attitude caused me to assume each relationship was going somewhere. I became possessive and expected more than the guys were willing to commit themselves to. And both relationships went the same place — nowhere.

We would do well to learn to have great friendships with men and not to expect any binding arrangements. Whether or not we marry, we are going to need male companionship throughout our lives, and the ability to be a friend to a man will help insure that we will have that companionship.

With friends a man will often open up more and reveal his real self. What an opportunity to learn about and understand men! Being a friend will prepare us to better meet the needs of any man God brings into our lives — a husband, children, a teenager at church, a man at work.

Friendships are to be valued just for themselves. Two people can contribute so much to each others' lives as each is willing to reveal himself and share what is happening in his life, his thoughts and feelings, and what God is teaching him.

Another problem often develops from hoping he's the one and acting like he is — sex.

Why does a Christian girl who desires to be a moral person get involved in pre-marital sex? There are a number of possible reasons.

First, there may be pressure from the guy. "We love

each other. Why not?" And if she is already hoping he's the one, she might agree. He may also apply the pressure from the world: "Everyone's doing it. Don't be old-fashioned."

A girl may have had sex when she was younger and is suffering from the mistakes of the past. Her desire for sex sometimes overcomes her desire *not* to have it.

But the main reason a girl will let herself get involved sexually is a desire to bind a man to her. When she gives herself to him, she feels that they belong to each other. She feels much closer to him — a part of him. And she believes it will give him the same feeling.

But sex often has just the opposite effect on a man. Rather than drawing him closer, he wants to run away. He doesn't want to be bound.

A friend shared with me just such an experience: "I loved him and I was sure he loved me. As we spent time together, we finally gave in to our desire for each other. Though I felt guilty for what we had done, I also felt much closer to him.

"Then the next night I saw him with another girl. I was crushed and couldn't understand. He had given himself to me, and now it seemed that he had taken himself back to share with someone else."

Relationships are often destroyed when two people play with sex. One couple felt they would probably get married, but then they slowly became physically involved. They hated what they were doing, and soon began to hate each other every time they had sex.

The relationships that stand the best chance of succeeding are those that limit, or avoid, physical contact before marriage. Of course, sometimes you will feel a need for affection — for someone's arms around you. Do you know some little children? One place to get some affection is from them. They have lots of love and hugs to give — and could use the same from you.

Another idea is to study Jesus. I see warmth and

affection in His relationships — love that comes from real intimacy. We can have that kind of intimacy with Him. And He can enable us to have the same intimate relationships with others that will help meet our needs for affection.

So we need to reject the backwards approach to dating relationships. We should stop acting as though each guy might be the one, but rather assume he's not until we know he is. The result will be more friendships and healthier dates.

6/ "I'm Made for a Man"

It was like a dream come true. There I was, sitting dutifully in my office, when this tall, blond, good-looking hunk walked in. He proceeded to impress me with his wit and his interest in me.

I was snowed. He took me skiing, sailing, picnicking in the mountains. We went for long walks. And he said he wanted God's will for his life. "Wow," I thought, "this is what I want." It was all too good to be true.

In fact, it was so wonderful that I wouldn't believe it at first. I had been hurt too many times before to take another chance. I prayed, "God, don't let me think this is real unless it really is."

But I finally gave in and believed that this could be it. I loved, and I even dared to think that it would work out.

Then the snow melted. He left my life as quickly as he had entered it. I was destroyed. Over the next few months my mood went from total despair to bitter resignation to grudging acceptance. I stopped talking to God — He seemed too cold and far away to listen. But finally my heart warmed up and I came around to trusting God again and believing that He loved me.

Meanwhile, this experience gave me more evidence for the case I was building. My life always seemed to revolve around a man. If I was dating someone, he filled my time and thoughts. If I had a crush on someone, I was always seeking to gain his attention. And if there was no one, which was usually the situation, I was looking for someone. Verdict: I must be made for a man.

I decided that I was meant for marriage. So I asked God, "What are You waiting for? Where is my man? Why do you always keep taking him away from me?"

I haven't been alone in these thoughts. A friend admitted, "I often feel that my time would be so much more meaningful and significant and enjoyable if there were some person into whom I could pour my life and time. I sometimes feel time is slipping away because I am without a focus, namely a man."

As I mentioned earlier, the natural desires that girls have to get married are encouraged and strengthened by almost everything we're taught. We become conditioned to believe that woman isn't complete until she's married.

One man told a 31-year-old single girl, "There must be something wrong with you, or else you're very unfeminine. Otherwise you'd be married."

Another man said to me, "Woman was made for man and isn't complete until she's married."

When I shared his comment with a close friend of mine, she replied, "If that's true, where is my man? Am I to spend half of my life, or maybe all of it, as only part of a person — incomplete?"

I agreed. When was God going to complete me?

When we cannot seem to find our fulfillment in a man, we look for it elsewhere. I sought fulfillment in my job, and it was rewarding. I looked for meaning through working with the teenagers in my church, and I really loved them. But I still felt I needed a man.

So that is what I told God. And He said, "Yes, you are meant for a man. You are meant for Me." That was startling.

Suddenly I knew that getting married was not what would fulfill me. My job wouldn't fulfill me. Helping others wouldn't do it. God Himself fulfills me — now.

The Bible tells us that the Lord has made all things for Himself (Colossians 1:1). Paul wrote, "And in Him (Christ) you have been made complete" (Colossians 2:10). That means whole and fulfilled.

If Christ is living in us, we are complete. He provides everything we need for living the abundant life He promises us, if we will allow Him to meet those needs. Yes, we are made for a man — we are made for God. He will bring people and things into our lives to add richness and depth. But that will not be our true source of fulfillment. It is only God who can complete and fulfill us — through Jesus Christ.

7/ "God's Woman for God's Man"

The Sensuous Woman, Fascinating Womanhood, The Fascinating Girl, How to Catch and Keep Your Husband Cookbook. Books on how to get your man in every conceivable way are in abundance today, and they often make the best seller lists.

Girls everywhere are eager for helpful hints in this area, although Christian girls are sometimes more "spiritual" about it. Favorite Bible study topics for single women include "How to Be God's Woman for God's Man" and "How to Prepare for Marriage."

I even heard of a seminar at a college retreat called "How to Get Your Man," including "testimonies" from mature Christian women who told just how they had gotten their men.

Understanding the role of a Christian wife is important,

and these seminars often provide vital preparation for this role that God has for many women. But often the primary premise girls get from many such studies is that marriage is a reward for spiritual maturity.

People tell us, "When you are spiritually ready, then God will bring that man for you. If you don't have a husband, you must still have some things to learn before God can trust you with him." So then we try to figure out what we need to do to be ready for marriage.

One girl said, "I had heard so many talks on marriage and prerequisites for marriage that I began to think that God would give me a husband only when I was spiritually mature enough. I began to try to learn the concepts that I had been told were signs of being ready."

A 26-year-old woman related, "As a result of a 'girl talk,' I decided to try to develop spiritually so God could bring my husband."

I was no exception. I felt that I had outgrown my childish attitude of thinking every guy might be "the one" and decided that I should become God's woman for God's man.

I thought about all of the attitudes that I should have. A wife should be submissive, I was told, so I tried to learn to be submissive. This did not come naturally to me, for I tend to resist authority and demand my own way.

My job, however, gave me opportunities to practice submissiveness (and still does). My suggestions were well received and my opinions respected. But sometimes the boss and I just didn't agree. In those times, he decided and I submitted.

I determined also that God's woman would be a woman of the Word; she would really know the Bible. So I began to dig into the Bible and study — another unnatural for me. I attended Bible studies and taught Bible studies. "Certainly," I thought, "I am beginning to become a spiritual giant."

However, the most important attitude to have, I had heard, was a willingness *not* to get married, if that were God's will. That was the hardest one for me. About the best I could do was to be willing to be *made* willing not to get married.

Supporting this spiritual self-improvement effort in my life was the favorite verse of many girls: "Delight yourself in the Lord and He will give you the desires of your heart" (Psalms 37:4).

We assume that if we do what He wants, He will give us what we want. What we want is to be married; so, theoretically, as we become spiritual giants, God will reward us with our husbands.

All of my second-guessing of God had some good results. I *did* learn to be more submissive, and I *did* grow as I studied the Word.

I wasn't the only one to have such positive side effects. "As a result of attending conferences and telling others about Christ," related a friend, "my faith was expanded, my prayer life grew, and I even read the Bible more as I searched for promises from God."

But this progress didn't necessarily get us any closer to marriage. In fact, as I looked around at many women — single and married — I realized that marriage and spiritual maturity were not necessarily synonymous.

This was made more evident to me when a close friend became engaged. She and a single woman who had been very important in her spiritual development were sitting together at a seminar when the speaker expressed this theory that marriage comes when you are "mature enough." The girls looked at each other and laughed, for it was obvious to both that the engaged girl was not the more mature.

I finally understood that I could not earn a husband. It is true that, when it is God's plan for us to marry, He will

work in our lives to make us the best partner for the man
He chooses. In this sense, we will get married when we are
"ready."

But a husband is a gift from God, given or not given
according to His perfect wisdom. We are married or
unmarried because it is God's will — not because we have
made "x" number of spiritual points.

Maybe you've never tried to become more of a woman
of God to catch a man. But have you ever looked at another
girl and wondered, "Why can't I be like her?" Or, "How
come she has so many dates?" Or, "Why is she married and
I'm not?"

When we're not satisfied with our "station" in life, we
sometimes begin to look at others and envy them. And
more often than not we short-change ourselves.

We begin to wear our hair the way a certain girl does.
Or try to tell jokes the way someone else does. Or develop
the qualities we like in another.

We can certainly learn from others, but we need to
accept and respect ourselves. We need to stop looking in
the mirror and saying, "Ugh! I don't like you and I don't
see how anyone else could either."

Instead we should be saying to the face in that mirror,
"I like you. Thank You, Lord, for making me the way I
am."

For God did make us the way we are — each for a
purpose. When we realize that God knows what He's doing
and that His plan is perfect, we can quit trying to be
someone else and be ourselves — the woman of God He
created us to be.

So what is a woman of God really like? The Bible tells us
that she has a gentle and quiet spirit: "And let not your
adornment be external only . . . but let it be the hidden
person of the heart, with the imperishable quality of a
gentle and quiet spirit, which is precious in the sight of God
(I Peter 3:3,4).

One woman said, "I'm glad it says quiet *spirit,* not quiet. I like to talk."

What is a gentle and quiet spirit? Does that mean you can never speak your own opinion? Do you have to meekly do all the dirty jobs and never get any credit for your work?

No. It means that everything you do is tempered with kindness. Because the God of all peace lives in you, you possess a peacefulness that holds you up when that man dumps on you, or the boss expects you to work over the weekend, or the bills are more than the paycheck.

With a gentle and quiet spirit, you get the job done, you express your opinion, but you do it without clamoring for attention — without saying, "See what I did."

More precious than gems — that's what a true woman of God is, according to a very wise man. See what he says in Proverbs 31:

She can be trusted. She's dependable. She will finish her work without the boss constantly checking on her. She'll be there to help when her family or roommates need her. She'll be honest, but with kindness.

She gets up before dawn. You must be kidding. What does she do that early? Spend time with the Lord, perhaps, arming herself with gentleness and quietness to overcome the trials of the day. Probably she eats a good breakfast to give her the strength she needs.

She is energetic, a hard worker. No just "getting by" with the bare minimum for this girl. No doubt she enjoys her work, because she knows it's for a purpose.

She watches for bargains. Thrifty. A good steward of what God has given her. She has nice things, but is not extravagant. And she is not tied to those things.

She generously gives to the needy. Realizing that all she has is a gift from God, she is quick to give back to Him and to reach out to help where people hurt.

She has no fear of winter, for she has made warm clothes. There's no drifting along here. The woman of God plans for the future. She looks at her goals and her needs, and takes steps now to be ready for the future.

She has no fear of old age. That's a hard one. "Grow old gracefully," the cliche says. "You're not getting older, you're getting better," says the ad. But God tells us, "Look at each day as a chance to accomplish what I have planned for you." Growing older just means that you're able to serve God with more maturity and fulfill more of His will for you.

Her words are wise, and kindness is the rule for everything she says. That cuts out a lot of my conversation. As women, we find it easy to say some not-too-nice things in such a nice way. Wise and kind — what good buttons for our lips.

Above all, the woman of God trusts God. She doesn't try to scheme to get His favor. She isn't always trying to figure out what He might want from her so she can get what she wants from Him in return. She trusts Him to work in her life to perform His perfect will. She wants to be God's woman — for God.

That should be our motivation for being God's woman. Not for a man. Not to be as good as someone else. We should want to be God's woman for God.

He is the one who completes us. He loves us perfectly. He gave Himself for us on the cross. He is the one we should desire to love and serve and please.

If we become all that God wants us to be, we will be equipped to serve Him and to be content with His will. Also, if we become all that God wants us to be, then we will be all that we should be for whomever God brings into our lives — a husband, friends, a Sunday school class, the elderly lady next door, the mailman or an airline stewardess.

God has a whole world — not just one man — that needs me to be God's woman.

8/ Libbing It

Isn't it amazing how it hurts — physically — when your heart aches? It's such an empty feeling.

After awhile, I found that I was tired of hurting. I had dreamed and had always been disappointed. I had given love and it had been rejected. I hated to see a relationship end, because that meant I would have to start over again and go through the pain and time of developing a new relationship.

To protect myself from further pain, I began to develop a new attitude, sort of a semi-women's liberation stance. I determined that I was completely independent and didn't need a man to fulfill me.

What I *really* meant was, "No man deserves all the love I can give him. Men are so undependable and untrustworthy that they shouldn't be as happy as I could make them."

So I began to build a wall around my heart. I stayed away from guys. I was hesitant to open up, lest I be hurt again. I became very independent. I didn't need anyone.

Of course, to buttress this attitude, I concentrated on all the advantages of being single. I had my independence and could do whatever I wanted to do and go wherever I wanted to go. I wasn't responsible to anyone else.

I once heard a married woman say excitedly, "My husband is going to *let* me get my hair done this week." I was horrified, and very glad I was single.

I especially liked not having to cook and wash and clean all the time. My roommates and I shared those jobs. I wasn't tied to the house by children. I could travel, which I love and have done much of — to Mexico, Europe, Hawaii, Israel, Korea.

Let's look more closely at some of these advantages of being single. They are real and should be considered strongly.

First, there are benefits that come from attaining a degree of independence. But many Christian girls, unfortunately, are afraid to become independent. They fear they won't be able to be submissive to a husband or won't be able to fulfill their roles as Christian women.

But there are many things to be said for being independent. You learn how to take care of yourself. You may be single all your life and won't have anyone to do your income tax or pay the car insurance or fix the disposal or earn a living for you.

Perhaps you will marry, but your husband has to be away often. He'll be much more comfortable knowing that you are capable of handling things at home. And, a married friend says, he'll appreciate your being your own person.

Or you may not have that husband all your life and will again be on your own.

The key, whether you are married or single, is that your ultimate dependency has to be on God. That will not change when you get married. And if, by being single for some time, you have been forced to become a very independent woman, God, when and if He brings a man along for you, will bring one who is strong enough that you will be able to respect him and submit to him in the way that you should, always keeping your dependency on the Lord first.

Many times a single girl also begins to take a leadership role in her work. But how can you maintain a gentle and quiet spirit and still be a leader?

Often, the men who are the greatest leaders are those who are gentle and quiet people. To be gentle and quiet doesn't mean you can't be firm — just not stubborn. It doesn't mean you can't be imaginative and creative — just not overly aggressive.

One man I know who teaches principles of leadership listed several characteristics of a real leader: commitment to a vision, a sensitivity to people, a willingness to make decisions and an understanding that you need to give before you expect something from someone.

None of these characteristics involves giving up a gentle and quiet spirit, yet these are the qualities of a true leader.

Another advantage of being single is that you will often have opportunities to discover yourself as a person, to develop an identity of your own.

How can we develop ourselves? We need to examine the various areas of our lives — mental, physical, social, cultural, spiritual — and decide what we can do in each area to become a more complete, more fun person.

Some activities don't fall into any category, and some overlap. But here are a few specific areas I have chosen for myself:

In my job, I am a writer and an editor. So I am always seeking ways to improve my abilities and excel in my work. Writing this book is an attempt to increase and expand my writing prowess as well as to share some ideas that have been helpful to me.

I have always preferred working with words and ideas to working with my hands. But two years ago the high cost of clothing and my desire for more creative expression forced me to learn to sew. I hated it at first (My roommates would laugh as I protested, "This is the dumbest thing I have ever seen. Why should anyone sew!"), but now I love it. And it's a special feeling to wear your own creation.

I also see cooking as a creative outlet and a chance to entertain. Learning to be a good hostess will be helpful throughout your life.

Maintaining our physical condition (and shapes) is important. Because I detest doing exercises, I've become an avid tennis player and bicycling nut.

Spiritually, I seek to develop my own study and prayer life. But one of my favorite experiences has been teaching a junior high Sunday school class for the past several years. I've been able to share some of my life with them, and it's been rich.

Your inclinations may be in entirely different areas, but never will you have as much time to develop your own personality as when you are single.

Then, if you do get married, you will take on an additional identity, but you will still be a person in your own right. What do I mean?

I can remember observing married women around me and realizing that I thought of most of them as "someone's wife." But I didn't think *I* wanted to be just someone's wife. I liked what God had made me, and I didn't want to give "me" up.

The married women I admired were those who were successful and fulfilled as wives and mothers, yet still maintained their own identities. When I thought of them I didn't picture just Joe Smith's wife; I also pictured Mary Smith. If I were to get married, I wanted to keep my own identity, too.

Another advantage to being single is that unique freedom to serve the Lord. The apostle Paul has something to say to the single girl in that passage most of us wish were not in the Bible — I Corinthians 7: "But the one who is married is concerned about the things of the world, how he may please his wife, and his interests are divided. And the woman who is unmarried, and the virgin, is concerned about the things of the Lord, that she may be holy in body and spirit" (I Corinthians 7:33,34).

This was the attitude that I consistently tried to maintain. I was genuinely concerned about the things of the Lord and wanted to please Him and serve Him. I was learning to be independent while depending on the Lord. I was assuming more responsibility and enjoying it, yet sought to keep my femininity.

A very close friend and I spent several months developing these theories on the liberated single woman. And, as I've said, I think the ideas are valid and can truly free a girl to be the woman God wants her to be.

But when my friend and I were really honest with ourselves, we admitted that often our motivation for being "liberated" was an underlying fear of being left out. Our independence came more from a fear of rejection than from a dependency on the Lord.

Fearing that we might be among those who do not get married, we employed an old football tactic — the best defense is a good offense. We wanted to face "old maidhood" early in our lives and become truly independent, rather than be caught off-guard and not married at 30 or 35 or 40, like some of our friends.

We wanted to convince everyone that it was good, as well as probable, that many girls would not get married. Then, if we never married, it would not look as if we were left out. It would appear that it was *our choice* to stay single.

Some of you may respond, "It could never look as though it were *my* choice to stay single. That's fine for you to become independent and avoid guys. But I never have any guys around to avoid."

Lest it sound like I have dates each week and have all sorts of men to avoid, let me clarify. I have never had an abundance of dates. Every relationship I've had since college has been mentioned in this book, some several times.

Nevertheless, I wasn't quite ready for the *results* of my attitude that no man deserved all the love I could give him. I went for more than a year without a date, and that was rough.

I spent countless Saturday nights feeling sorry for myself. A girlfriend had a record called "Everybody Loves Saturday Nights," which we would play and then laugh — and cry. Many times when I saw happy couples together, I was jealous and miserable.

And yet, as time went on, I found that there were a lot fewer frustrations than when I was dating someone. There was no one to fall short of my expectations. I didn't have to wonder if things would work out the way I wanted them to. And I didn't experience the pain that comes when a relationship ends.

I learned that I could get along without men in dating or romantic relationships. And as I saw that I could live without them, that I didn't have to have a man to love, I realized also that there was a way in which I could give the love that I so much wanted to express. I discovered how to give that love which said, "I'm made for a man because I want so much to love one and to wrap my life around him."

I learned that I could give my love to God. I had loved Him before, but that was primarily on an intellectual and spiritual level. It was not with my complete being, not with my emotions.

I learned to be in love with the Lord Jesus, and I realized that spending time with Him could truly satisfy my desires and meet my needs right now. Talking with Him about ideas, problems, thoughts and desires could be as real as talking with a close friend, and even richer. Reading His Word and learning about His character enabled me to begin to see things more from His perspective, and often caused me to laugh at some of the things I saw in my life that had seemed so important before.

And so I began to be very satisfied that I was in His hands, that I could trust Him. I knew He was in control and that He was someone who always loved me perfectly, and who would always accept my love. I began to date some again, but many times I have been able to apply the principles I learned about depending on God and yet being independent, about serving Him wholeheartedly, about showering my love on Him and rejoicing in His love for me.

9/ You Better Believe It

What attitude should a single girl have? She needs to realize that "old maid" is a dirty word (really two dirty words — one dirty thought). That is, no woman should consider herself an old maid. The term implies that her singleness is a negative condition. But being in God's perfect will is far from negative. There is no better place that we can be.

The key is simply to be in God's will. All through this book I have talked about knowing God, trusting Him, being fulfilled by Him. How is this possible?

I grew up believing in God and that Jesus was His Son. I believed Jesus died for our sins and assumed that everything was okay between God and me. Then I learned that it wasn't enough just to *believe* that Jesus died, was buried and rose again. Forgiveness for my sins was a gift which I personally had to *accept*.

Jesus promised that, if I would invite Him to come into

my life as Savior and Lord, He would forgive all my sin and give me eternal life (John 3:16,36). He also promised to give me the full, abundant life He had planned for me (John 10:10).

So I prayed — talked to God — and asked Christ to come into my life, to forgive me and to take first place in my life.

He did come in, and He kept His promises. This book is the result of some vital things I have learned as I have sought to keep Him in first place — to trust Him — especially with my singleness. Which brings us back again to old maids.

Being single is not being an old maid. It is a special calling, even as being married is a special calling. It is part of God's plan. Just as I have brown hair, am an American and am a woman, I also happen to be single.

One of my friends told me how she got her attitude about being single straightened out. "I finally believed that God hadn't forgotten me," she said. "Being single is just part of His plan for me."

Many people spend their lives getting ready to live and never get around to living. Rather than concentrating on the Lord and serving Him, we are more concerned about whether a certain man might be "the one." We look expectantly around every corner in hopes of finding that man.

We view our jobs as temporary until a man comes along. We look at life as though the future and perhaps even the past were more fulfilling than today. We remember wistfully or we dream hopefully, but we despair of the present, for there is no man in the present.

Let me share with you a letter from a bride of one year to one of her girlfriends:

Your question: "Why is it that fairly often it seems like the things I'm involved in are just things to fill time until I meet the man who will cause all the regular, every day stuff to have significance?"

Answer (rather, opinion): You feel that way because you're human. You're made to be hungry for a man — or something of significance that you feel like putting your time into.

But even after you get a man and even get married, you'll still be hungry. Because you're human and on your way to Christ-likeness, you will always have a spark of restlessness in you. I still have it, as happy and settled as I am with my husband.

I still wish for something else to do, for better days, for spiritual progress in my life. That restlessness is part of being alive. Sometimes it's almost gone when you've discovered God's next step in His plan and you get all settled in a niche.

But the feeling comes back and when you're single, it's easy to put your finger on the absence of a man as a cause. That may be true at that point because God is making you, or rather allowing you, to want to settle down. But that doesn't mean that when a man comes, the restlessness will go away.

You'll always look ahead and want more — not in a discontented way, but in an expectant, thirsty way. You'll want more of what God has, more of what He wants to teach you.

When I got married, I thought I could and would put all my time into my husband and thus feel fulfilled. You know what? That never worked. Because he is a servant of the Lord, he couldn't and wouldn't want to put all his time into me. And because I was his partner, I had to put a lot of my time and energy into his ministry, and especially into all the other people in our life together. In other words, we shared each other with everyone else.

But our time wasn't wasted when we acknowledged that it was the Lord's. It *was* wasted when I'd want him all to myself. When I make him my god and the center of my life, it's rotten. He hates it and I do, too. But when Christ is at the center, we're both fulfilled.

It is time to stop considering the present as a temporary state of affairs — as merely preparation for the "real life" ahead of us. The present is fulfilling.

When we do find ourselves despairing, God has provided some clear instruction for us: "Don't worry about anything; instead, pray about everything; tell God your needs and don't forget to thank Him for His answers. If you do this you will experience God's peace, which is far more wonderful than the human mind can understand. His peace will keep your thoughts and your hearts quiet and at rest as you trust in Christ Jesus" (Philippians 4:6,7, Living Bible).

But what about the loneliness that will never leave you alone? Even when your attitude is right, the loneliness can stay. You can, of course, follow the standard advice — plan activities with people; take up a hobby or project that really draws you in; become involved in helping others. These are good remedies.

However, think also about what you can *gain* from loneliness. Jesus was lonely — He was single for 33 years. He was often misunderstood and rejected. Use your lonely times to get closer to Jesus, to see more of what He was like, to become more like Him. And realize that your loneliness will enable you to feel what others feel and help them when they need comforting.

Jesus said, "Do not be anxious then, saying 'What shall

we eat?' or 'What shall we drink?' or 'With what shall we clothe ourselves?' (or 'Whom shall I marry?' or 'Will I ever marry?'). But seek first His kingdom, and His righteousness; and all these things shall be added unto you" (Matthew 6:31,33).

The essential attitude is faith — trusting God. Without faith it is impossible to please Him (Hebrews 11:6). Anything that is not of faith is sin (Romans 14:23). Therefore, lack of faith hinders God from working in our lives.

What I am going to say now may seem to contradict what I've been saying so far, but actually it doesn't. Just as we must trust God to meet our needs and fulfill us without husbands, so we must trust Him to give us the man He has for us, if that is His will.

Let me explain. Often, as girls pass 25, they begin to feel that God has forgotten them. They move from *expecting* God to give them husbands to *doubting* that He will. They resign themselves to being "single and satisfied." Or they even doubt that God loves them enough to give them what they really want.

But God doesn't want our resignation or fear or doubt. He wants our trust. Just as we are not to assume that we will get married, also we should not decide that God is going to withhold a husband from us.

He has said that, even as human parents don't give stones to their children when they ask for bread, so He will not give us bad things (Matthew 7:9-11). He says that He won't withhold any good thing from those who walk uprightly (Psalms 84:11).

As I said earlier, most women will get married. If you are not one of those, then God will still fulfill you. Trust Him. Trust Him to give you what you need. If your desire is to be married, then trust God to fulfill it or to change it. Let Him hold your desires and wishes in His hands so they do not overcome you.

When those desires do begin to overcome, consciously

give them to God. When those thoughts begin to fill your mind, displace them with other things that are true, honorable, right, pure, lovely, of good repute, excellent and worthy of praise, as Philippians 4:8 tells us. Claim for yourself II Corinthians 10:5, ". . . taking every thought captive to the obedience of Christ."

In seeking to trust God, however, we often get mixed up about the object of our faith. We trust Him because of what He has promised or because of what He's already done for us. We trust Him because of what we want Him to do or expect Him to do. But we're to trust Him because of *who He is.*

And who is He? He's God, the creator of the world; "In the beginning God created the heavens and the earth" (Genesis 1:1). He asks, "Where were you when I laid the foundation of the earth?" (Job 38:4, Living Bible).

He is just, yet merciful. "The judgments of the Lord are true and righteous altogether" (Psalms 19:9). "Your throne is founded on two strong pillars — the one is Justice and the other Righteousness. Mercy and Truth walk before You as Your attendants" (Psalms 89:14, Living Bible).

He is wise. Daniel said, "Blessed be the name of God forever and ever, for He alone has all wisdom and all power" (Daniel 2:20, Living).

And He is our loving Father who has a perfect plan for each one of us. Jesus said, "For the Father Himself loves you dearly because you love Me and believe that I came from the Father . . . God showed His great love for us by sending Christ to die for us while we were still sinners" (John 16:27; Romans 5:8, Living). Paul tells us that the will of God is "good, acceptable and perfect" (Romans 12:2).

Can we trust a God like that? If we really believe that He loves us and has a perfect plan for our lives, then we can allow Him to control us and believe that He knows what He is doing. We can be truly and totally committed to the Lord Jesus, for it is He who makes us complete.

And this works. One 31-year-old friend looks at being single as a privilege: "Although I would like to get married, it doesn't frighten me at all that I might not. I consider everything as a gift from God and can hardly wait to see what else He has for me."

No man can complete us totally or understand us perfectly. Just ask those who are married: "I expected my husband to fulfill all my needs, and he couldn't," said one woman. "As a result, we both felt like unfulfilled failures. Then I put my eyes on Christ and let Him meet my needs. Now we are both satisfied."

We are complete in Christ. As we trust Him, we can live now — in the present. Because God's will is perfect, it is for now, and it is fulfilling today.